Lines
Written a Few
Miles Above

Andrew Peters

Other titles:

Natural Light, 2018
Edge of Light, 2019
Wavelengths, 2020

2023

Ingram Spark

To Ed,
Family
and Friends

TABLE OF CONTENTS

First Light

The Long Walk

Night Calls

First Light

7

Among Things That Grow

When the evening news becomes too human
and light slants over the hill,
I go outside to sit with things that grow
and listen for birdsong trills
that settle the unsettled air
and remind me of all I do not know.

I go out to see the green buds show
their reminder of winter's end,
to watch them imperceptibly grow
even when I'm not there.

I go to hear the birds sing songs
they know all over the world,
sing despite my presence,
despite all that is wrong.

Oh the raging world is never too far,
it circles round and tries a way through,
but among the blameless living,
I breathe a breath of truth.

And while I am there
with all the shining green
that makes for us every living thing
even when we don't care,
my heart feels a little less broken,
and my soul, a little more whole.

When the evening news is too human
and light slants over the hill,
I stay outside with things that grow
and watch the stars appear

and breathe the air so clear.

Simplicity

It is all so simple really.
Here a gentle breeze
wafts from the heat
of some distant sunlight
shaft like an outstretched
arm about a shoulder,

when just there afloat
like a tiny filament boat
sets sail a migrant seed
with microscopic architecture
millennia in the making
with a charter to start
a new dandelion generation
in some loamy patch,
risking a withering
among cold stones.

It is all so simple really
this single delicate seed
of a dandelion weed
carrying futures of untold bees,
of untold animals and plants
across the lands
and even into the seas,
all waiting for that single seed
riding the wayward breeze
to settle to a hopeful thatch.

It is all so simple really
watching the seed drift
like a hundred others unseen
through the rifts of time,
watching all that is sublime
unfurl in patterns of life,
wind stirring hair and leaves
and feathered light.

Intersection

In languages hence as in long ages past,
there is the small space,
the single thought like a wall
covered with whispering mirrors,
whispering as if time were forgettable.
That small space refuses breathable
entrance and clings to shifting
darkness moving the uncatchable dream.

But there are truths
that soar feathered and ethereal
into expanding orbitals
that sweep pulsing instants
into a plane of being,
time into matter,
motion into moment.

The simplicity of light
in all its wavelengths
is not the fabric itself,
but illumines every intersection
where gravity becomes
perceivable beauty,
the wordless instinct of joy

rising through despair
like vermilion shafts of dawn
out of night.

Lepidoptera

The chrysalis opens and beauty
self unaware emerges wet
with rebirth unfurling
genetic memory, color
in the language of wings
ready to float the first breeze
in search one by one of flowers.

What Cretaceous thought set
forth such tender fragility
a role essential to propagating
greenery of the world?
What helped its tender survival
through the catastrophe
that left so many extinct?

Whispers in great diversity
fill ever-changing, remaking
earth with nucleic solutions.
An uncounted billion insect lives,
uncounted billion insect deaths
have led to this gossamer song
that now traverses garden scenes.

This my plot planted for me,
this fleeting breath of one brief life
now inherits a visitation
as of long lost friends whose deep embrace
only old care-worn hearts understand,
hearts that always hold remembrance.

The brief life of this butterfly,
but a few months long, now meets
this flower that wilts in days.
Neither know millions of years
of lifetimes lived,
nor do I comprehend ancestral paths
through fires and floods,

migrations and homesteads,
wars and passions,
heartaches and joys felt,

yet here am I
part of this life-bound meeting,
witness here and now to beauty,
present, undeserved, to this greeting,
present, undeserved, to this beauty,
present, undeserved, to this peace.

Homeplace

My uncle ran the homeplace dairy
just off the two-lane highway
a few miles from the family cemetery
we've left behind.

Some years I got
a month in the country
shared with cousins.

All-day expeditions outdoors
we'd wade the grassy fields
watching aimless cows
breathing Oklahoma dust
swirling in the ceaseless wind,

and we'd walk the stream
along its wanderings,
hunting turtles, avoiding snakes,
testing quicksand banks,
splashing through shallows
to find some new way
deep in the cottonwood sway.

I learned languages that have no words,
rustlings and whirrings,
tongues of animals and birds.
And I discovered unclocked time
following the irregular sun
in slow passage over the plain.

When we needed importance
we'd battle an army of orcs
with wooden blades,
or vanquish a quested dragon
to save the long besieged.

And when in need of repose
we'd climb hay bales in the barn

to sort out all
that since goes unremembered.

When the days were ripe
we'd eat mulberries
in the wide shade of the tree
old as the farm
and hope at lunch we'd find
a fresh-baked pie.

When evening came with cows afield
we'd join the herding to bring them home
for the evening milking.

Later after games we'd play,
sleep would finally overtake me
and I would dream the dreams
children dream, imagining heroisms
being an adult changing the world,

not knowing then how day by day
choices would come large and small,
indistinguishable, sliding past
like leaves in a stream racing.

Debris

Face to face with themselves,
lines of age exposed
like fissures in granite
just past the last quake,
finally, finally there is
nothing left but awake

to think at last about
living not for fear,
not for unlived beliefs,
not even for the peace
that breathes through
the unforgiven past,

rather to think
            about
the long slide of tears
unseen into jumbled debris
ready for the smooth touch

of wind and rain
over jagged edges.

Forest Silence

After noise of traffic ebbs,
quiet night arrives
like an old, troubled friend.
Sitting in the darkened forest
what matters escapes
like the long sigh
of the fading sun.

But even here, even here
there is no lasting silence.
Just-now rustles among fallen leaves,
and high up branches creak
wooden metaphors of forgotten dreams.

I have asked them in their woody wisdom
what there is about the crafted blade
at the end of the long handle,
what so irresistible to labored hands.
But I hear only stoic silence
that reverberates axe-wise
to a splitting of my brain in two,

wondering what consciousness is alive,
and who lives the senseless
natural disaster.

Gather Moments

Boulders tossed randomly lean
unsteady as a walk in strong currents.
Having found places for rest,
their imperceptible potential
appears balanced and controlled,
but ask the quiet trees
whose forty-foot friends
lie broken and brown.

Their whispers describe a time past,
a time to come when none in heaven
or earth know the direction
of destruction, when questions
have no answers.

Gather then moments like gems,
they suggest, matching this one with that,
gripped tightly in the tentacles
of roots. Arrange and rearrange them
by color, place and memory,
not only those broken from cliffs
whose jagged edges open wounds,
but also those worn smooth
as river stones who shape impressions
in the silt of distant deltas,
all sparkling in beams
when the sun is bright,
when the moon is full.

Gather moments they whisper,
for stringing and restringing,
the way life slides quantum choices
along endless vibrations of songs,
spinning across spaces,
rippling double-helix twists
when the moon is full,
when the sun is bright.

So living runs like cascades
down altered paths,
altered again.   Perhaps
the course of the stream bed
doesn't matter to the boulder
after the slope has claimed it
and splashing enters
the inevitable lake.

Or all the stones exposed
in upturned roots are like
angled light off stream-cast spray
where knowledge and beauty
meet in the sparkle of eyes
and the gentle roar in ears
and the cool air that brushes
the edges of the face,

as though there are feathered wings
that hope to find seeds
on an open, outstretched hand.

Wading

The stream is clear here
where smooth stones
shine like gems
and the waters whisper
so there's no feeling alone.

The water is always cold,
colder than the fickle air
and when wet reaches hems
most of the wandering years
slide away in the silver rush.

I have been there
where the current is strong
and wading uneasy.
I have seen the waving fish
unfazed by the power
that pulls feet aside.

Sounds from the land on either shore
are unheard here midstream,
and all that seemed so vital before,
now is here a casual dream,
reasons for crossing, a postponed wish.

The unbalanced struggle to cross
calls attention to every move.
I have been there and danced on moss
and managed to find a way through.

Sitting to dry on the far shore
I have wondered where
all the water finally flows,
finally far away goes.

Words

They sit in their rooms
writing, writing, writing
          as if it mattered,
gazing up to the left,
fingers curled around pens
scratching the surface,
            ink sinking in,
or now again looking off to the right,
fingertips clattering letter to letter
            on keys electric.

They sit in their rooms
writing, writing, writing
            as if it mattered,
which, of course, it does,
just as wings of a huge flock,
fluttering like wind-tossed pages,
            take off
on a great migration that changes
            the world;

or like the bee drifting by
in search of a field of flowers
as provisions for a hive feast,
            not knowing,
how daisies and penstemons
and berries and fruits
            rely on its busy visits,
not to mention cattle and deer
and rabbits and wolves.

And what they write
            cuts deeper
than swords, proclaims freedom
            and equality,
when they get around to it,
usually after a polished mirror,

or mythic icon,
or after a riot is calmed
or stirred up.

And what they write
describes the world,
tanks passing by windows,
and the aroma of bread
in the morning,
and gentle children at play, curious,
and all the lost and lonely adrift,
and joy bursting from celebrating throngs
like flashing lights,
and strength that climbs sheer cliffs,
and silent tears of sorrow,
and darting fears of scattering prey,
and the intimate look from sidelong eyes,
and crouching tigers and soaring hawks,
and dunes of heat piled dry
in drifts,
and the glistening at night
of rain-drenched streets.

And what they write
arises from casual gravitons
and photons in cosmic drift,
arises from amino salts
intended
by plummeting asteroids,
arises from the DNA of thought
and the plasma
of all that is felt.

Sometimes they sit at desks
writing, writing, writing,
or sprawled among scattered sheets,
now and again
gazing out the window
at tornadic clouds
moving in gray-green,

or in the variance of time
at clouds brimming
            with vermilion evening.

They sit in their rooms
writing, writing, writing,
            as if it mattered,
which, of course, it does,
just as the word of creation
            whispered
in galactic spirals
            knots
the fertilized dream
of salmon to the nitrogen web
that feeds bears, and trees,
and algae in the wide,
            wide seas.

Meadow

Whenever I notice the birds are gone
along with their songs,
I begin to gather
things, just a few, rather

and when engines roar
up and down the streets,
I begin to think where to go,
and where to go farther,

and when the news is full with war
and flaming hatreds soar,
I leave and lock the door
and though I mean to be discrete

with packed up mind I run
into the forest of gentle trees
and knowing what I know
of wolves and bears

and all the warm-blooded problems there,
off I go with less to fear,
heading for a certain meadow
where gathered in the waiting glen

flocks and flocks of churring cranes
stride among the living world in peace.

Skipping Stones

Along every stream I met,
boyhood feet wandering,
stones were thrown for effects
of plunge, rings expanding
around rebounded peaks,
ring after ring, wider and wider,
all too soon reabsorbed
into the water's expanse,

then some year one day
I learned the trick
of sideways skipping,

thereafter at every lakeshore
of memory if winds weren't stirring
waves too rough for learning
I would find flat stones to set
between thumb and fingerings
just so to sidelong spin
flat surface to flat surface,
stone grazing watery face,
hopping two, three, four times,
or there nine, and there eight,
and there was it twelve I think,
each creating rings expanding,

and what is memory really
but the surface of the soul
as moments drop through
setting rings to quiver
their sense of meaning
and sometimes sidelong
to skim a path across the edge
of what we think we know.

Gladness

I would embrace strong limbs
holding me close to the sky
and look the knotted eyes
in the eye breathing the green
breath of leaves.

I would dream boyhood dreams
of dangers surpassed and fears
vanquished, of kings and queens
and knights with no peers,
lonesome for all the good done,

dreams all clinging to ridged bark
smelling the cool shade,
hearing the rustling dance.

And I would stay the day
in my own private ark,
learning secrets of sap,
smoothness of cambium,
seeing the heartwood and pith
of broken branches

until time for meals
or when the reclining sun
would coax me in.

I was glad for those days
of unmeasured time,
glad for the ways
I learned the rhyme
of wind through limbs
and flickering leaves.

And I am glad still
though climbing is done,
glad for all the between,
springtime flowers of dogwood,
redbud, and apricot,

summer fruit from apples,
pecans and peaches,
autumnal brilliance in red
and yellow, maple and oak,
sweet gum and aspen,
and the careful way
snow lines limbs
and ice hangs from ends,

glad for walks among majesty
in the steadfast shade
of ancient bristlecone,
sequoia and pine trees,
glad for the living
that captures light
and everlasting breeze.

Shines the Stream

Silver shines the cutting stream
through steep walled canyons
and living dreams.

Wildness approaches the shore
soft as footfalls of memory,
wary of boisterous screams
echoing off granite stanchions,
echoing off visions of the stream,
water sluicing mineral wealth, as victory.

Silver shines the cutting stream
through deeper canyons
of unconscious mystery
fed by thunderous storms
whose rains find hidden faults
that wedge out great blocks of thought
to crash the canyon floor,

and what was conjured long ago,
vain as the passage of time,
is found to not
be what it seemed.

Silver shines the cutting stream
whenever angles rise
precipitous and cascades
become a deafening roar
impressive as mountains of myth
before unavoidable mudslides
and rockfalls irretrievably
find narrows far below,

and grain by grain
whatever was missed
or believed someday to be
is carried away to dark and distant seas,
leaving only smoothed and weathered faces.

Holy in Darkness

They sit on the dock
stooped over, knotting
and reknotting their nets,
intent on the net
and on all those knots,
catching strands,
bringing them together,
managing ties with the grip
of ancient fingers deft
with practiced wonder.

Here and there they test
the strength of it,
pulling strand by strand
the tautness of webbing,
the surety of cords.
Survival depends on the net,
families, communities,
civilizations in need of fish,
silver hope for the future.

Totally in focus, they cast
their nets into water,
leaving patterns on the surface
as the webbing sinks, soon drawn up
again full of the precious feast.

Repairs are always required
as weaknesses are exposed.
They sit on the dock
stooped over, knotting
and reknotting their nets,
intent on nets,
not on the vast darkness
of waters passing through.

Mystics dream of the strand
by strand knotting

connection after connection.
Across the millennia
they build holy places
oriented in the patterns of stars.
At night looking up,
Orion's belt, the wings of Cygnus,
scales of Libra, horns of Taurus
must mean something.

Somewhere out there
embedded in the cast
of mystical dreams
imagining patterns of light
a vast darkness passes through.

The

Long

Walk

The River

The river bed varies
by depth and silt
and covered stones,
solid outcrop or broken gravel.

Shallow the water unravels
a rainbow spray.
Deeper the placid face
belies propulsion
unrestrainable
unquenchable.

The vast terrain,
mountains, hills,
and rolling plains
are circumstance,
cause for the roiling dance.

Boulders and bends
are moments presenting
every element of choice.

Looking back up river
it is always unclear
whether the river chooses
its way around boulders
through the landscape
or whether terrain
shapes the water's course
or whether gravity
like an unseen god lives
through the river's
unconscious belief.

Way Home

It is dark and home is far away.
The heart calloused to suffering
is empty, the mind, silent,
but hollow the voice
echoes through city canyons
off brick and concrete and steel.

The pleading of music pounding,
rough and loud in smoke-filled rooms
grows louder with the sound
of glasses clinking, louder
on busy streets crowded
with the sound of feet moving.

Across the land such souls
are pressurized vessels
ready to explode at a touch.
The din of their heedless talk
is like whitened bones clattering,
clattering together in the rattling wind.

It is dark and home is far away.
With silent screams from lonely glances,
long shadows disappear into the night.
In darkness long questions, unanswered,
become layers of doubt and fear
hardening the autonomous shell.

In darkness all that has been lost
collapses to a blind singularity,
eyes and ears searching the unsearchable.
The question is imagined at last
whether the moon will rise,
whether day will ever come.

And among echoes deep beneath surfaces
time unlived drips as though from stalactites
into life-ebbed caverns of sorrow.

It is dark and home is far away
across the rugged face of earth.

Yet even in darkness the migrant mind
fearless unblinds windows in the night,
to witness life moving into every niche
in search of sustenance and sanctuary,
lives that live unexplained.

Across the rugged face of earth,
humility settles like morning dew,
manna for the vagrant mind,
and gratitude leavens the waiting heart,
setting phosphor memories glimmering
in the early light of dawn.

Shafts of light sweep angular paths
tilting shadows to new points of view,
and there across the rugged face of earth
the humble heart raises a sanguine flare
and eyes stirred by gratitude
awaken on the confluent sublime,
awaken on home ever present, ever alive.

Across the rugged face of earth
the air breathes long breaths of hope
soft as green sprouts, soft as the air stirred
by eyelashes as they open
on the green boughs of home,
home among rushes along the blue shore,
home among scattered outcrops of stone,
among fields and prairies waving their gold,
home wherever wings can fold,
home wherever life grows old.

Ode to a Stump

The body, it can be told,
will become the softness
of moss.

There in the glen,
within the fallen
all the rings of life
lose their lines to frass
that fades softer and softer
in the hollow core
into the humus of yesterday,
the peat that feeds
the forest of sapling roots.

What of the mind
and all those memories
beautiful as the green sparkle
shifting in the gentle breeze,
beautiful as translucent shine
holding, holding the sun
to its covenant.

Beyond the glen, the light
unfailingly shines
and an unfolding
rustles and whispers
with the drifting
aroma of pine
long through the moonlight,

all the distant, radiant points
embedded in the memorial night.

Drought

dry, the earth cracks a puzzled 'scape
lonely for watered care

life struggles there
stifled in the summer air
when all the green has ebbed away

after a timeless time
after brittle leaves drop
noiseless to the ground
inevitably comes a rain
in gentle mist or raging storm
that clears memories away

and life finds a way
                                 again

I have been there
adrift in stifled summer air
when all the green has ebbed away

I have walked the walk
from a senseless grave
with no idea where
life might begin again

but after a timeless time
after brittle thoughts break
in furious drought

comes the cleansing rain
relentless in bringing change
unpuzzled to ever living life

and green grow new shoots
from old branches and limbs
singing old hymns

and deeper grow roots
deeper into precious earth
into humus ready for birth

Softly comes a calling
as from a sheltered place
waiting.

Softly comes a calling
as of feathered mornings
glistening with dew waiting
for open eyes to see
emergent buds and tendril roots
like the gentle urge of belief.

O the longing grace
that lives a rarified world,
untimed and unpaced,
that risks a thousand ways
to find one that lives revival
and joy in each discovery.

Softly comes a calling
as of a passing breeze seeking
listening ears to hear
the songs sung by trees unrivaled
like the tender thought of hope
deep in the chlorophyll of leaves.

O the creative grace
living the diversified earth
that makes of chaos and discord
the sense of harmonic form
that grows in waves of vibrance
like the elegant beauty of faith.

Softly comes a calling
as of a childhood trance
that doesn't know the dance
but finds moves and rhythms
that quell persistent fears
like the community of hymns.

O the brilliance of grace
living the dangers of space
that makes of death
the very means to persevere
in every adapted sphere
like the timeless presence of love.

Softly comes a calling as of a dove,
settled to evening peace,
awaiting the coming gloam
with resolve in folded wings
as if it is possible to know
the point of survival.

dark their eyes and troubled
they come with a great rattling
in the to and fro of wagons
down a narrow road rutted
from years of common use
comes the caravan of blues

taste of dust on their tongues
dust in every breath
no great flashing tragedy
to elicit universal sympathy
never in the evening news
just the pallor of faces
reflected in unseen places
souls like worn out shoes
comes the caravan of blues

wasn't always a caravan,
never imagined that was the plan,
but one by one they came
never two sorrows the same
day by day walking through ashes
of what was once a passion
never arriving forever leaving
endlessly adrift in grieving
but now have nothing left to lose
comes the caravan of blues

they take joy in the masquerade
camping on the outskirts of the mind
to plan the nightly parade
waiting for dark and drinking wine
they sew clothing of every shade
dyed with broken hearted hues
with highlights of sparkling jewels
whose every facet is a flash
of bygone joy locked in the past
for the past is the only news
on the caravan of blues

they've never a thought for fame
knowing what differs in being the same

they have given up knowing
for the whelming of being
ignore importance for showing
that losing can be freeing
because they've seen the ending
and there's no pretending
on the caravan of blues

some days, memorial days,
their music can be heard, the way
the aroma of baking bread wafts through
an open window with the breeze
that can be so soothing
but when darkness draws close
and thoughts begin to freeze
in the cold of that night air
there can be an aura of despair
and when you feel most morose
then comes the caravan of blues

and the music is near,
            notes more clear
and in the fire
            of their desire
they dance
            oh how they dance
                as if in a trance
along the edge of a forgotten hum
that you may have thought was numb

and in the whirling round
sparkles are enwrapped with sound
until the sun begins to rise
      to the opening of eyes
      that still find surprise
and you have a way of knowing
in the end you've made it through
with the help of musical truths
from the caravan of blues.

Perdido

That song was a song I couldn't forget.
Oh some of the words, even bars
of melody, some are vanished or dim
but I haven't forgotten how I felt,
irresistible that swing,

like that day on the mountain lost
without paths or cairns,
nothing but blue sky and peaks,
an eagle cry echoing away,
the peace of the swinging trees.

I have sought that old song years on,
musical score or simply lyrics,
but only found spurious recordings
done by hacks and imitators.

So perhaps it is truly lost
in the pathless wanderings of time
and if found by now would not be the same,
its sense eroded away.

Or perhaps the truth of it now
lives only in me, rhythm driving my heart,
refrain dancing through veins,
old harmonies shaking vocal cords.
Perhaps its intimations
are hidden in the meaning of words
I speak or even imagine.

Like that lost peak from long ago
that may have crumbled for all I know.
That song that I remember,
now lost to ears gone deaf,
still burns a living ember
in the deepest beating chamber
that in this heart warms enough.

That was a song I couldn't forget,
irresistible that swing.

Stain

The hero is you and me
among the thousand faces
gifted with identity.
Failure and mystery lurk there and there,
but the soft grin is true,
glimmerings in unmasked eyes
worth the ebb and flow,
casual coffee shops brimming
with long winds of debate,
eventual resolutions to justice,
and visions of peace,
and rallies in town squares
with swaying crowds singing themselves
to unison, each one wielding
favorite super powers,
seeking the greater good.

But thousands of years of masks
dancing around fires have also led to this,
the stain that is the lie,
obfuscation of aspirations
assumption of possession,
polluted visions of meaning.
The stain, fingerprints embedded, corrupts.

Masked, the visage looks to self
for answers wasting all that survival.
Masked, the visage doesn't see
the stain spreading into the streets.
Masked, the visage claims to be unmasked,
that unmasked are masked.
Even now the stain spreads
deeper and wider, vivid in cities,
but spreading too down every dirt road
proud of its lineage.

Drop by drop the stain issued
from the head of Abel,

drop by drop down centuries of lies
denying all the questions
hanging from the stars.
Masked hands still hold nails
ready for piercing now
the feet of truth all over again,
drop by drop issuing
from the pierced side,
century by century answering
questions with inquisitions,
spreading the stain wider, deeper.

What Promethean thoughts
imagine grace to be
civilized and captive
within walls of doubt and fear?
What flame kindled for earthen pots
now illumines forges of war
and careless thoughts of violence?
What thoughts imagine wax wings
might course the breath of earth sunward
as proof of existence,
forever in the dream-bound rush?

Stories and stories grow from minds
masking the human truth,
as if it were too late to stem
the widening stain, drop by drop
widening the between
that closes thoughts and hearts.

Like islands of plastic
infiltrating ocean life,
the stain, fingerprints embedded, spreads.
And like clouds of smoke from great fires
burning earth's tender crust,
the stain leaves landscapes bleak and dry.
And like unforgiving floods that creep
then flow with irresistible force,
the stain sweeps away vestiges of peace.

And like diseases insidious within
that destroy cell by cell and move on,
the stain consumes the living truth of life.
The stain has changed the world.

But perhaps it is not too late,
not too late for wordless stories
and thoughts unmasked to wake
from dreams of unlimited life,
dreams of unlimited wealth,
to awaken lost hearts to beat
with the rhythms of breathing earth.
Perhaps it is not too late to touch
the rim of seasons and sense
the sun-bleached shore.

Cairn

Early on a cairn appeared, smooth stones
shining like dew across the meadow,
some stones dark, some light, composed
in a stack by a clever hand
rare and artful whose meaning
deftly balanced meant more
than any words I knew.

And so a pause to assess
what path to take or leave alone,
what way might be forged.
No path continued straight on
none to directions left or right,
no grasses bent as if trod,
nothing unsettled in sight.

I wondered what the stones suggested,
the author's intent, so studied
the lovely granite lines,
sparkling quartz like glistening eyes
I couldn't resist.
I waited as if it would all come clear,
but the sun on rising burned hot,
so step by step I made my way,
each day a new world,
each world a new day.

Many are the years traversed,
many the worlds lived
rough, lean, plentiful, rich,
heart broken and full
in wonder of life
in all its heroic chance,
like the flash of fireflies
when comes the gloam,

but have found few cairns since
that have inspired,

none so artful in design.

I too have left cairns along the way
not for memories that end with me
but for a future hope that some
might question the view
and perhaps find something to see.

I still wonder what happened
to that early cairn,
why I found no other,
but the beauty of those stones,
the angles they posed
have been the grain of sand
now pearled in my soul.

Headless

Childhood ends in a moment,
    like a twist
of grandma's strong hands,
    the expert slice
through the neck
    and the chicken
headless flopping
    endlessly flopping
around the bloody yard.

At last then plucking
    soft feathers away,
and the smell of singed
    death at last
before it becomes
    a meal.

The gruesome truth
    cannot be hidden
by batter and grease,
    but follows everywhere:

to bloody-nosed school yard,
    to a reckless generation
and even to a nation
    flopping around headless

losing blood.

<h1 style="text-align:center">Few Words</h1>

I will be of few words
for though they once gathered round
like faces shining in the dark
now they twitter or scowl,
turn away preferring the mystery
of some curious distance.

Once they ran
like children hand in hand,
whipping their play
into long sentences
and stories, glorious
in their mythology.

Now their whitened bones stand,
stoic as ruined temples,
columns broken and scattered.

Where have they gone,
invisible in day-blind silence,
whispering like vagrant winds
over watery surfaces?

To see them at all,
hear their difficult wisdom,
there is only the night
when they appear,

passing in and out
of the windows of dreams,
as stars in red-shifting reticence,

as if in search
of forgetful infinity.

Fog

The fog rolls in
from parts unknown,
could be the wide, empty ocean,
or from restless mountain slopes,
or dew rising in the morning
after a night asleep in the field.

Like a blue marauder
it obliterates thought
but heightens senses
to search dim forms of trees and stones

for anything that moves.

In the stillness time slows
and breathing grows thin.
In the closeness I hear whispers
of things I can not say,

memories never made,
stories never to be told,
lines of rhyme no one
will ever read.

Dense fog comes and goes
leaving portents
of nevers and forevers
dripping from weary branches.

The spiralled shell
gives up hope,
mind busied in exigence,
reason lost in silence.

Yet still the resilient heart
remembers to beat
its measured frame
as if to regulate mystery

in fearless waiting
for some new realized clarity,
what will appear
when the sun burns away

the blindness of living.

Fissure

up on the hill
close to the pinnacle
the weathered boulder
is cracked wide open
darkness deep in the fissure

like thousands of others
exposed to the elements,
inevitable erosion and decay
workings of the entropic blade

such fissures never heal
like so many hearts
broken from disaster
and disease, left to silent
mourning in the moaning wind

memories like dust
settle in the dark between
ready for some unexpected seed
to shift topology
sending forth some new edge
in search of light

Trumpet's Refrain

The old horn sits the shelf,
river of song silenced
long ago before the young heart
knew how long expedience
might hold captive the truth.

It might seem that old self
could be given up for lost,
yet within the movement of art
something ignores the cost
of living the narrow dance.

How can now an old heart
understand the river- cut gorge,
echoes fading along the rim;
how can what remains be forged
when memories begin to dim?

Among countless melodies ruthless
in cutting the steepness of meaning
something about one, always one,
pulls deepest the deep being
down and down the misty abyss.

What holds now the slowing heart is this,
the indelible memory of a refrain
once so common, now among the lost,
where breathes the final pain
with no regard for timely cost.

No, the old horn presses not the lips
that might play that song renewed,
for gravity allows no second chance,
and finding where the truth once grew
exposes rim to rim a vast distance.

Hallelujah

Stars in wandering cold nights
have no need for hallelujahs
and yet they are there.

Owls in flight through dark woods,
eyes wide in silent search,
hear no hallelujahs
and yet they are there.

Among the migrant lost
where all have been,
dreams of home
dream no hallelujahs
and yet they are there.

Along the moonlit shore
crabs scrambling over the beach
have no thought of hallelujahs
and yet they are there.

Among homeless tents,
shuddering the cold night through,
there are no secret chords of hallelujahs,
and yet they are there.

Aerie steeps echoing with raptor cries
echo no hallelujahs,
and yet they are there.

Indiscriminate snows covering the earth
shift on the crest of winter air
without hallelujahs
and yet still they are there.

Among those whose labors
allow no thought but labor,
or those whose pain
allows no thought but pain,

allows no hallelujahs
yet still they are there.

Among forests of pines
the wind sings its needled songs
without voices for hallelujahs,
and yet they are there.

Through marbled halls and rooms
lavishly furnished no tiles ring
with chords of hallelujahs,
no minor fourths, no major fifths,
and yet still they are there.

Handel saw no Christmas star,
no grazing sheep
except in dreams of mind
from whence came dreams of hallelujahs
springing onto noted scores,
springing thenceforth across generations
of voices young and old,
hallelujahs upon hallelujahs.

Do you fear the windswept storms of night,
or shiftless, dreamless days?
Do you fear violent destruction,
and the coming end of age?

Listen
for rustling wings in flight,
jazz tones that stir your mind.
Listen
for running feet and shifting leaves,
blue notes that ease your heart.
Listen
for songs in ocean deeps,
orchestral chords that caress your soul,
and even the silence you fear,
for there are hallelujahs
ringing in every ear,

glistening in every living eye.

There are no angel choruses
no robes of light,
unless galaxies swirl with stars
and yet still from quarks
near the beginning of time
to the nearest niche,
the closest breath,
from farthest reaches
of lonely thought
to the nearest instant felt,
still there are hallelujahs,
hallelujahs upon hallelujahs,

for those who have ears to hear,
let them hear.

Night Calls

Alarm

I

The alarm sounds,
    harbinger of the new day,
call to the rising moment,
cacophony of wings and songs
    lifting potential
to the freeborn sigh of dawn.

Fogged, the mirror tells
a different story in black and white,
    gray of time long past,
wrinkles of the long-passed year,
languid breath of the vanished dream.

Surely it will be there
    when the mist clears,
    day of the new breath.
Surely the mirror will reflect
    robust thoughts
waiting to begin an ungrayed day,
    day of lines smoothed.

The day begins anyway,
a day like all others
    unlike any others
that will not resurrect old myths,
    not relive old days of ungrayed hair,
just a day seeking clear eyes
that might survive.

II

The alarm sounds
    when a boat appears
    along the coast,
harbinger of global tragedy,
    slowly, at first so slow,
the sky fills with black wings
    circling,
    hunting the breath of life,
carving lines along veins
    of pumping blood,

veins of commerce
between living and dead,
between gasping truth
        and fear of isolation.

The morning mirror adorns masks
        that hold the dark truth
        of survival.
The mirror doesn't lie
but reflects only
        who we are with our
        unreasoned hope
an unmasked dream,

going forth to remake the day
        newly immune to the dis-ease
that divides us from the rest,
going forth to find some way
        to survive this dis-integration.

III

The alarm sounds
        when glacier after glacier
slides into oceans
        at the ends of the earth,
harbinger of change,
        slowly, at first so slow,
the sky darkens with storms
        power unmeasured,
and reefs in the deeps
        begin to die,
and flames tower over forests,
        rushing to turn green
        to black and gray ashes
floating the superheated breeze.

The morning mirror fogs
        in dumbfounded silence,
        shaken by the truth
of self inflicted vicissitude,
        disclaiming the fault
that now reverberates
        Marianas to Everest,
hoping outlines

59

of artful gray
will lead somewhere else,
        to some new day
invented by the genius
        of youth,
some child who has unlearned
what was never known

until the point tipped past
        too late
questions survival.

IV

Alarm! Alarm! the days
        slip away!
An excess of mirrors reflect
        themselves
at two-dimensional angles
that set the world ablaze.

Surely it will be there
        when the smoke clears,
a day of new breath,
an ungrayed day,
        a day of lines smoothed.

The day begins anyway,
a day like all others
        unlike any others
a day that will not resurrect
old myths nor relive old days,

        a day to be made
        in revival.
Tal vez tenemos tiempo.

Reciprocity

Sitting on the back porch
coffee in the morning chill
I see them now
perfectly aligned
        LaGrange points,

negotiation and argument
        in orbit
suspended without a crash
without flying off
        to empty space.

Could be anything
        any argument
        any negotiation,
siblings lovers partners
enemies rivals fans.

In orthogonal silence
        between points
each in their own path
        balanced
without worry of intercept,
where words assume pleasing
            shapes
of solved equations,
parabolic reflections,
fractal memories,
quadratic hopes.

Coffee in the morning chill
I see them now
perfectly aligned as wings
        of a dove
at rest after a long flight
over choppy waters.

Solution

Shapes like spirals spinning
the personal web at last turn fractal,
for example the obsidian blade
polished like a question
never answered.

Rain is coming they say
and with it hail
and chances of tornadoes,
hurricanes and flooding,
but there is no belief,
proud of the era achieved
where all things are but choice.

I was the problem all along
thinking to figure it all out
just takes time
and willingness to back away
for larger views,
never considering consequences
of living daily ease enamored
with technological wonders.

I so loved seeing the city
from the boat, just a captain
and I setting out to look back
at skyscrapers rising up
along the shore,
water leading to shining metal,
glittering lights at night.

Now looking back I wonder
what will happen to bones
of the city, all that metal
all that concrete
all that wiring
when earth reclaims
its right of eminent domain.

And I was right of course,
figuring out just takes time
and the wider view,
which of course is the problem,
thinking time and distance squared
would be enough,
thinking sometimes
it is fractional proximity
in diminishing integrals,

or thinking at all
when all it takes,
seeing up close the cutting blade,
listening to the fractal spin afar,
is understanding how it feels
to see the skyline sinking.

Almost Home

Close to home now the roads are rutted with age.
Trees lining the way,
leaves covered with dust fifteen hands high,
drooped limbs as if a welcoming embrace.

All the things that led so far away
long ago are now vague
as dusk, urgency past,
firefly choices blinking in the haze.

Not pushed out in petulance,
as leaving the gate open,
lured by curious indecision away.
Reasons for leaving,
now ill-considered excuses,
are better forgotten,
like fields plowed under.

I remember those who'd gather
on the lawn in the darkling eve
and talk out the passions of our days
for the betterment of all.

We'd watch the birds bob on the wire,
those I swore to follow when they flew,
but never found in all the wheres.

I have been away too long.
Fields need their turning,
but now I am less inclined
for civilized rows,
and so will let go.

Now here are landmarks, childhood in reverse:
the stream once splashed and waded,
learning to fish and swim,
now dry gulch in changed times.

Here's the road that learned to drive,
and the ditch that stuck the car
when once was struck with some diversion.

Here's the one-room school in disrepair
before my birth, and the little church
abandoned long ago
for what I would never know.

Here's the copse now overgrown
that always held it's secret peace,
and close by, the clearing
where bonfire stories folded arms
into the silent night.

Here's the wide field we would walk,
and ah, there's still a circling hawk,
circling still the upper heights.

Closer now, over that rise,
the turn,
and I wonder about all the eyes
and smiles of a lifetime,
and about tears and fears,
and I wonder what needs
the next generations for stories.

Would that there be greetings
and music and stories at the end.

Embedded

In greening leaves the song changes
from minor keys of leafless winter
to open stops gleaning the sun's gift

sparkling the singular flash
embedded in the ubiquitous
across a thousand surfaces,

like intricate melodies
finding a way through the resonance
of harmonic chords.

Early slanted tones
rise up soft on gossamer wings,
soft as cool shades.

I have heard them
streaming among branches
filtering carbon timbres
with refrains.

In the vibrant course
that flows in rays
in briefness of days
there are answers
to all that goes unasked.

There may be why
birds sit the branches
to sing in dappled shade,
where listening leaves me
breathless as Bach.

Heart and Mind

I would have thought by now,
weathered and wrinkled,
my mind would be clever
as ravens in congregate genius,
and heart tough as raptors
soaring above the painful earth.

But no, heart and mind,
together at last,
seem delicate as the lesser goldfinch,
obvious as cardinals
perusing the snow and ice
of winter landscapes,

wary as the titmouse or chickadee
darting branch to branch
flying quickly tree to tree,
or as the hummingbird suspended
as if somehow the inevitable
might be escaped.

Pursuit of Meaning

Finally after all these years
a picture window large enough
to see off into the night
where distant the city lights
blend indistinct among the stars.

Now visible the steady pursuer
approaches again,
crafty persona plodding sure
along whatever path taken,
carrying that worn-out satchel
full of tired questions
and cold memories,

crafty persona that takes no breath
but rides every exhale
like seeds on the wind,
seeing everything and nothing at once,
hearing every sound into its silence,
moving among shadows in wait,
fearless for it carries the gleaming
sword of love.

When did pursuer become pursued?
When from youth when notes
left to golden-haired weave
brought close the meeting of eyes,
green of earth with blue of skies,
when in tumult of exigencies
and blind passages
did pursuer become pursued?

Now in haze of evening
through the window approaches
the steady pursuer cloaked
within old thoughts of life.

What will happen once I am found
here out of breath,
heart slowing,
bones creaking,
as darkness closes in?

Endings

The flame that once cut
jagged edges in the dark
and reduced the cold
to harmless shivers

now, now declines advance
and diminishes like whispers
in the wind, whatever said
all too soon forgotten.

Embers pull down the flickering heat
as if tying sails to orange masts,
ready for the calm.

This is it then
as folks have drifted off
carrying stories to homes
in well-worn leather.

This is it then
for the fire cannot be reversed
to leave logs fresh
any more than years can return
to youth.

This is it then
for I have declared
clear cutting done,
and the woven tapestry
of these stories have found
their blackened endings.

I watch the final glow
with ash-smudged brow,
hands facing the escaping warmth,
thoughts set adrift to wander
among the stars.

There is still the chance
like the fresh breeze
that stirs calm waters
to snatch a happy moment
before it is gone.

Who dances the next world to being
will not know stories I see
now floating as sparks
disappearing in the night.

They will write something new
for another night, another flame
that will arise in gathered eyes
passing new stories among them
in the widening circle of light.

Now embers have earned
their slow silence,
the hush of their vapors rising.

This is it then,
the solitude,
unavoidable solitude
that comes late,
the truth that glows
before the cold
at the end.

Remember Me

When you walk paths among the trees,
remember me to the gentle breeze
that shifts the shafts of gold
between the leaves.
Say I still long to hold
that light and all that air.

When you sit in garden bowers,
remember me to all the flowers.
Say how much it always meant
to breathe the freedom of their scent.

When you chance to brave
a midnight walk along the shore,
remember me to the rolling waves.
Tell them how I miss the foam
and the moving sand between my toes.

And when the birds return to nest,
tell them how I loved their song,
but could not stay so long,
for it came my time to rest.

Taps

Hosts of polished marble and cut stone
in shades of gray rise up row on row,
raising up chiseled names and dates
and other unwritten mysteries.

Waiting, trumpet in hand,
I would sit among those shades of gray,
and read the pithy epitaphs,
regard the flowers in their fabric,
some fresh, some wilted,
some eternal in their plastic.

And I read the spans
subtracting to know the ages:
July 21, 1915 - October 2, 1943
February 4, 1897 - May 16, 1965
August 11, 1960 - January 18, 1961

Among those measured terms of life
most were elders which to youth seemed fair,
younger seemed more tragic,
                    though all
were but a blink in human history,
history but the quickest flash
to epochs stretching millennia
into hundreds of millions of years.

And how many creatures large and small
have come and gone none can recall?
What purpose all those living moments
of beings now long extinct?

I would wait in every season,
sometimes in drizzling spring,
or in beautiful summer days,
but I always felt more right
in winter bundled against the cold,
fingers icy on the horn.

I was always early as needed
for the playing of those familiar notes
to give the gathered ... what?
comfort?   finality?

Waiting, I would see fresh dirt
piled a short distance and wonder
how slabs in shades of gray
might keep us honest,
taking nothing for granted,
gripping each moment
like polished brass ready
for the tones we breathe.

The procession would slowly appear,
hearse first parking near,
and somber faces indistinct
would circle the awning
behind honored seats.
Soft the murmurs I couldn't hear,
but waited for the signal

and I would play
the old traditional tune
ending the day,
ending the life,
me the living pretense
                    of Gabriel.

On through life I suffered
good friends their passing
                    and parents,
each in their way, leaving
where I could not follow.

Each passage reaffirmed
a human belief of purpose
that death makes life worth living.

And now,
now cascades of the river Styx seem near
and passages of time less clear,
and perhaps we're meant to cherish
    our brief span

and maybe it is life's long plan
against the chaos rampant universe,
against chance of random dissolution
to achieve enough diversity
of form and genes to insure survival
against entropy and perversity.

Gravity

In every memory shines a star
pulled in orbit round the galactic heart,
and among the circling paths
conjunctions pierce the empty dark,

like a song unbidden heard
on random occasion that recalls
a certain place and time, songs
I played in spotlight on stage,

songs I sang in a car
driving dimly lit roads, songs
sung to quiet the wakened babe,
a bird that sings a mournful call.

Another alignment appears
when in a nearby field children run
with a kite and suddenly I'm there
running with a kite, you holding
the string spinning off the spool,

and then I'm holding the string
and you run until the kite lifts
higher, higher caught by the wind
holding us taught together.

Then another, sitting alone
in a quiet house surrounded
by shelves of books and displays
of rock-bound crystals

suddenly I'm on a desert hill
surrounded by chalcedony florets,
geodes from ancient volcanic flows
we sort and heft into bags,

and suddenly I'm sifting a rocky slope
surrounded by species long extinct

held in trembling hands,
vivid in discovering eyes.

On a rainy day, drops cascading the panes,
I hear other sounds of rains,
heavy on canvas roof,
gentle on umbrellas raised,
feet splashing sidewalk pools,
huddled voices in makeshift shelters.

Again in casual passage seeing a flower
freshly bloomed, I see mother
clip backyard roses for a special day,
and irises for a table display,

and I see a special corsage,
and then a spring bouquet,
and there are flowering trees
and gardens at home and afar
and also mounded sprays,
all aligned in paths circling
round the galactic heart.

A darkness, forgetful darkness
widens between the sparks,
quiets the busy thoughts,
stills the quickened beats,
but does not affect the gentle pull

that draws patterns in the stars,
myths within the meaning.
I lean toward the unknowable core,
the light I cannot ignore
in hope for an event horizon
that can scrape clean
all my unintended harms.

Hollow No More

I

We are the masters of progress,
conquerors of doubt.
We are the masters of innovation
experts in the science of change.

We gather by the numbers in cities
in jubilant celebration of all we know,
all we have done, all we plan to do.
Our vastness is recorded

and copied for the ages to come.
We send our messages out
to the universe to any intelligence
who might wonder who we are.

We are the masters of progress,
conquerors of doubt,
who fear nothing for we have
endured the violent century,

which has left us unparalleled,
for we are between nothing,
and nothing is between us,
we who do as we please.

We are the masters of change
unafraid of those sharp teeth.
Knowing what we know
of evolution we string bows

and send our arrows
        into the future,
we who have ended doubt
in favor of obsession.

We who have tamed change
through rampant compulsion,
have conquered fear of nature,
now fearing only ourselves.

II

Hollow no more
        the figures run
    along forbidden shores
free of being

no longer hollow crushed thin
        in the century
            mad with violence
mad from the rush of wealth

believing the quashing
        of hollowed spaces
        makes fewer impurities
and leaves no grieving.

No longer hollow the figures pace
        flattened hallways
            with flattened thoughts
pressed into pixilated life

disbelieving regrets
            need be redeemed
wherever meaning is dry
        as cracked earth.

III

Hollow no more
        figures wander the surface
of stages set for soap-opera dramas
        and mass market movements

fearful of added dimensions
        comfortable with two
        like Sistine memories

that leaves a guessing

thinking simplicity is enough
        for deathless reruns
of painless pleasures
        and painless violence.

No longer hollow but twinkling
        in ordered lines
in screen-wise believing
        in recordings echoing

vibrant messages to farthest
galactic revolutions
        as if some Star Wars story
explains everything.

Hollow no more
the figures meander through
        the graveyard of emotions
as if sorrow weren't enough the first time

as if joy might be relived afresh
as if the meaning of the story
        might be changed
upon quantum reading

a difference of perspective,
        of possibilities
from the surface
        of the collapse.

Give us Barabbas they say.
Give us the violent way
        for those who cower
        have no power

and we are masters of today.

IV

We are the masters of evolution,
we who have made of the apple
dozens of varieties,
we who have found a use for us

of every natural feature, every resource,
     knowing ways of DNA synthesis
now having formed the world
     of our dream,

needing no kingdoms beyond
for we have made a deathless home
     shaped in shimmering lines
     along the indifferent shore.

We are the masters of creation
     having made reality
into ideas floating back and forth
     in glittering time,

singing the popular scream
     on crackling screens.
Having found death's dream kingdom,
     we have no need of sight

with all the glitterings,
     and nothing from death's gray,
nothing from what we say
is irrelevant or untrue

     or even unassumed
in our self-defined truth
like the shell of bombed out cities
when power finally finds its due.

V

Hollow no more reduced
     a dimension

leaving only faith and hope
        without the synergy

that makes divinity
        relevant
that might just save
        the world if only,

if only Gestalt were true,
if only a wafer careful
on the tongue would ignite
        consuming fire

among the detritus,
that clears the expanse
        of fields and forests
        for new seeds to root.

Hollow no more if only
        the blinding presence
of the distant sun might shine
on the chlorophyll of soul

and bring forth leaves from flatland soil
like the music that echoes
through spires of hope
        as if the plain fact is

that there is meaning after all
like continental drift
over the mystery deep beneath
        the magma of thought,

mystery that spins the global
        presence into beautiful
patterns when eyes open
        like the explosion of flowers

on a dimension reclaimed.

Fear not for blessed are the cold peaks
and blessed are volcanic fumaroles
and blessed is the crest

    of the wave on the sand
    in unplugged hush
that smooths footprints and castles
making visible empty shells

and breathing holes in the strand.

Psalm Two

Every bone cries out for you,
O Absence of Thought,
from the yearning in my soul
whether deserved or not,
for I would hold what is true,
would believe and be whole.

Where are the bright edges of your eyes
that saw through my darkened frame
before fate settled over me
like dust on a mirror,
and I, complicit, drifted away
wrapped with exigencies in search
of comfort and ease.

Where is the waving sheen
of your hair that circled the sky
in ribbons of gold;
where the endless care
that found me in my despair
when I was lost and alone?

Mine was the muddled leaving
                I know,
mine the promises unkept
you never wanted anyway,
now long since past what wept
in busied solitude.

The more I stare
into the memory of your silence
the more I am blinded.
Bring me the muddy paste
made holy by your touch
                for
you have been the vision
in my quizzical eyes,
hearing in my catechist ears,

breathing in my sultry breath.

Yet, O Dream of Presence,
unnamed hope for what might be,
I know you are everywhere here,
                    for
you are the dark in night,
and you are the light in day,
and you are the chime
before bells are struck,
and you are the sound in the striking,
and the resonance after.

Like a fish in water
which cannot name water,
mine is the compulsion,
mine, the obsession for swimming
                    ceaselessly.

Now every bone cries out for you
O Spark of Being,
every creak and crack of joint
reminds me of the wisdom you
told me long ago,
that nothing of this matters
but those we come to know
in unimagined insight,
                    for

you are the heart of my heart,
yours the sense in all my senses,
yours the tears in all my grieving,
yours the joy in all my living.

Holy Spirit

I know you are there
    somewhere
drifting in and out
    light as air

in your usual ungrasped way
    speaking without
voice to say
    the shifting day

is enough, always enough
    to quell doubt,
to bridge the gulf
    earned in rough

passage of despair.
    I remember that night
that felt so wide
    and the tide

that carried me away
    that lonely night.
I had nothing to say.
    I had no right.

As a youth there,
    in the lonely light
of far-flung stars,
    I begged you to appear
from the vague dark
    to somewhere near.

I sought the assurance
    you cannot give
for there in the silence
    where I have to live

you are as close
        as my heart,
your words close
        as flickers
in the glimmers
        of my mind.

I know you are here
        somewhere
drifting in and out
        light as air
in the taste of my mouth,
        wind in my hair,

knowing the beauty
        I have seen,
knowing the pain
        I have been.

Deeply Interfused

> While with an eye made quiet by the power
> Of harmony, and the deep power of joy,
> We see into the life of things.
> ...Tintern Abbey -- William Wordsworth

"Radical pessimist" they say,
but it just won't go away,
the heat boiling my head,
the thought of extinctions
like the ache in my knees
with the possibility the next twist
will lay me down,
      lay me down.

It just won't go away
how nothing comes from clouds
but the memory of snow capped peaks,
dim in gray mists,
caliginous as dreams
I gave up long ago,
      long ago.

But it's also the fires,
fires scorching the sense of hope,
sooted faces dripping sweat,
proud for the few homes saved,
proud standing on cindered hillsides,
blackened trees, branchless, crisp.

It just won't go away
the silence in my heart
with nothing to say,
      nothing to say.

When I was young
and steeped in meliorism,
wrapped close in warm thoughts,
all the babble made sense,

babble growing to technobabble
when they said going to the moon
proved anything can be done.

Now it just won't go away
the plastic waste lining shores,
plastic strewn on forest floors,
billions of seeds scattered
across concrete lots.

It won't go away
the look in wild eyes
unsure what to do
        where to go
a little frightened,
        a little lost,
scattering grass to rock,
banging into glass panes
with white-tipped wings,
flattened on busy freeways,
off somewhere dazed
not knowing why,

and now I am almost as ready
as the wolves and lonely bears,
almost as ready
as the screeching hawk
and scavenging fox
and all the others,
just about ready
looking to the sky

ready to shuffle the deck
and start over,
        start over.

"Radical optimist" they say
but they just won't leave me alone,
paths with no end
questions without answers,

   urges to go,
   urges to know,
clear-eyed clouds whose harmonies
remember all the songs
that spin round my mind,
spin round my mind.

They pull me along,
rolling numbers like waves
   over the shore,
an unbound throng,
pi to 300 and more,
symmetries that appeal,
fractal places that know no wrong,
equations working working
   to perfect balance,
geometric shapes forming
symphonies that float
like the ammonitic whirl of galaxies.

They pull me along
brief melodies in birdsongs
like hands under armpits lifting
that repeat, repeat,
like the sounds of wind
through pine needles,
the crash of waterfalls,
the rush of water curling
  into sparkling foam,
then into the unending silence
  of fog.

They pull me along,
the gaze intent
of dogs expectant
and the quizzical tilt
   of lizard heads
and the mystery of the turtle
withdrawn into its carapace.

They pull me along
green edges of leaves unfurling
their sparkling flags of freedom
as if they, the Kingdom of plants,
discovered long ago
the secret chemistry of hope.

They just won't leave me alone
the eyes of this and that child
wanting to know now,
dancing in the light, spinning
one moment, seeing something
new the next, singing
loud and strong and the tears,
oh the tears that beg
for one more, ringing,
so true,   so true.

They won't leave me alone
the eyes of this and that child
because they know
        the way home,
a new way they've made,
like important seeds
        they find
they really want to plant
because they have to believe,
        have to believe.

I am radical they say,
but there's another way
I've come to believe
in the seamless fabric
        of symmetry
and all that is simultaneous
like sore muscles growing
        through pain,
and arthritic joints
that have to move,
and the moments, precious moments,

when love and sorrow
        join in grief.

I've learned, at once
the whiffs of longing and home,
the lift of baking bread,
with the yearn of distant rain,
serenity of gardenias
filling the room,
with the drifting aroma
        of blooms,
like honeysuckle and wisteria
filling the open air,
filling the open air.

I've come to believe
in the impossible elegance
        of wings,
for I see the sun rise
day after day
like a rose among thorns,
day after day
lifting thick mists
off forested shoulders,
day after day pulling up
fresh blooms as if in the end
come what may
it will all be okay,
like being in the shade
of the twisted arms
of the live oak.

And I see the sun grace
wind across ocean plains,
and sparkle on the peaks
of leaping waves,

and day after day
I see the sun, come evening,
like a rose among thorns

settle blue mountains
with a tight tuck
of shadowed covers,
hazy peaks disappearing,
ready for the night,
ready for the night.

And like a rose among thorns
day after day I've learned
the unsympathetic
knowledge that time
is relative, all gathered moments
of quantum plasma,
like reflections of faces
on the surface
        of a lake,
there and not there.

And like the voice I heard once
        long ago
soft as falling snow,
white through barren trees,
I have come to believe
in the simultaneous speech
in the moment, brief
moment when the end
is the beginning.

9 798218 131944